Straight Talk, Straight Walk
Practicing Spiritual Disciplines

Dr. Maxie Miller Jr., D. Min.
Senior Pastor, New City Church of Plant City
President of M-Cubed; Maxie Miller Ministries

Copyright © 2016 by Dr. Maxie Miller Jr., D. Min.
Cover Design By: Dr. Maxie Miller Jr., D. Min.
ISBN: -13-978-1530796342

Edited By: Dr. Lynn Spivey, Ph. D.

All rights reserved. Reproduction or translation of any part of this book through any means without permission of the copyright owner in unlawful, except for promotional use by individual contributing authors or book reviewers who may quote passages in a review in print or online, as long as the following statement is included:

Excerpted from Straight Talk, Straight Walk: Practicing Spiritual Disciplines

Request for other permissions or further information should be addressed in writing to:

Maxie Miller Ministries
1808 – James L. Redman Pkwy
PMB #307
Plant City, Florida 33563

Although every precaution has been taken in the preparation of this book, the publisher, the author, and the contributors assume no responsibility for errors or omissions. Liability will not be assumed for any damages resulting from the use of information contained herein.

Table of Content

Biography 8

Introduction 12

Disciplines of Abstinence:

Solitude 20

Silence 20

Fasting 24

Frugality 29

Chastity 34

Secrecy 38

Sacrifice 42

Disciplines of Engagement:

Study 48

Worship 52

Celebration 55

Service 59

Prayer 61

Confession 73

Submission 76

Conclusion 79

Prayer Journal & Note Guide 80

Bibliography 90

Dr. Maxie Miller Jr. is a native of Birmingham, Alabama. He was called into the gospel ministry in 1980 in Albany, N.Y. He retired from the U.S. Air Force in 1990 after 20 years of service. He is a graduate of St. Leo College, Tampa, Florida where he earned his B. A. degree in 1980; he completed a B. S. degree in Religious Studies from Wayland Baptist University in Honolulu, Hawaii in1986. He completed his Masters of Divinity degree from Beeson Divinity School of Samford University in Birmingham, Alabama in 1995. He earned his Doctor of Ministry degree from New Orleans Baptist Theological Seminary, May 2011.

He has over 30 years in the ministry. He is sought after for his knowledge of the Word and his ability to assist Pastors in the areas of Church Growth, effective evangelism, Sunday School growth, financial growth, revivals, and community ministries.

During his tenure as Director of the African American Ministries Division, Dr. Miller was responsible for giving leadership to the Florida Baptist Convention's ministry to over 3 million African Americans living in Florida. He pastored churches in Utica, New York; Colorado Springs, Colorado; Birmingham, Alabama and Plant City, Florida.

He was elected 1st Vice President of the Florida Baptist Convention from 2001-2002; served as Sunday School Growth Consultant from 1997-2002, elected as the first African American Moderator of Shiloh Baptist Association from 2001-2002, member of the Florida Baptist Witness Commission from 2000-2002, and President of the Board of Directors, Pregnancy Care Center of Plant City from 2000-2002.

In 2011 Dr. Miller was the first African American to be voted as Interim Pastor of Cedar Grove Baptist Church, Plant City (an all Anglo church) where he served until a Pastor was installed. In June 2011 he was the subject of a profile in the Florida Baptist Witness titled "Godly Men, Preaching to Every Tribe, Nation & Tongue."

Dr. Miller's published Dissertation: *Equip African American Ministries Division to Reach Florida's Unchurched African American Population Through Church Planting* was released in 2011. He has written the forward for Dr. Tony Evans book *Oneness Embraced* and testimonials for Pat Williams, former president of the Orlando Magic, which appeared in his book titled *The Difference You Make*. Dr. Miller has also published two workbooks: *Tools for an Effective Prayer Life* and *Enhance Your Obedience To God* - Practicing Spiritual Disciplines.

Dr. Miller is the President and Founder of M-Cubed – Maxie Miller Ministries, a Consulting firm designed to assist churches and leaders with their ministry needs.

He currently serves as Senior Pastor of New City Church of Plant City, Florida, where his ministry targeted audience is to reach the lost regardless of age or ethnicity, and their compassion audience is to reach the Hip-Hop culture with the Gospel. He is a member of First Baptist Church of Plant City.

Introduction

The world seeks to destroy our witness. Many leaders, presidents, teachers, pastors and Christians have fallen, yet redeemable, but they have lost their witness. Our faith in God is not a walk of diminishing return. God has expectations for us which are rooted and grounded in our faith in Him, "... what we will be has not yet been revealed" (1 John 3:2). The challenge Christian's face are to learn how to live as representatives of God. Paul records in Romans 12:1-2, "I beseech you therefore, brethren, by the mercies of God, that ye present your bodies a living sacrifice, holy, acceptable unto God, which is your reasonable service. And be not conformed to this world: but be ye transformed by the renewing of your mind, that ye may prove what is that good, and acceptable, and perfect, will of God. As Christians, we have one life to impact a lost world with the Gospel; we have one day to be change agents in this world: this day; and we have one moment to make a difference in the life of someone for Jesus sake: this moment.

God has redeem us for the purpose of worshiping Him, representing Him, and leading a lost world to the saving Grace of Jesus Christ. Therefore, Christians must protect their witness. The hour is far spent, and time is short; we cannot afford to allow our witness for the Lord to become weakened by our fleshly desires.

Christians are to represent our Lord, no longer presenting life as a picture in a frame, beautiful and nice to behold, yet spiritually lifeless, not obeying God's Word. In the Epistle of James one of the major problems in the church was a failure on the part of many of the Jewish Christians to live what they professed to believe. While other problems existed among Jewish believers, James concluded that the common cause of their problems was *spiritual immaturity*. The basic theme of James is *the mark of maturity in the Christian life.* James used the word "perfect" several times, a word which means "mature, complete" (James 1:4, 17, 25; 2:22; 3:2). By "a perfect man" (James 3:2), James did not mean a sinless man, but rather one who is mature, balanced, grown-up.

Identifying spiritual disciplines that will usher Christians into a closer journey with God may be more subjective than objective. Scripture is a positive beginning point. Peter records that the believer has a progressive call on his or her life, a call from God to take the next step:

> But to obtain these gifts, you need more than faith; you must also work hard to be good, and even that is not enough. For then you must learn to know God better and discover what he wants

you to do. Next, learn to put aside your own desires so that you will become patient and godly, gladly letting God have his way with you. This will make possible the next step, which is for you to enjoy other people and to like them, and finally you will grow to love them deeply. The more you go on in this way, the more you will grow strong spiritually and become faithful and useful to our Lord Jesus Christ (2 Pet. 1:5-8, LB).

The ultimate aim of spiritual discipline is to bring believers into an effective cooperation with Christ and his Kingdom. Dallas Willard explains, "When we understand that grace (*charis*) is a gift (*charisma*), we then see that to grow in grace is to grow in what is given to us of God and by God."[1]

The objective of understanding and practicing spiritual disciplines is to assist you with your spiritual

---

[1]Dallas Willard, *The Spirit of the Disciplines* (San Francisco: Harper Collins Publishers), 156.

diet. Spiritual disciplines have as its primary aim to bring us closer to our Lord, in humility, will, and purpose.

The spiritual disciplines channel believers to God's grace and to the practice of His gifts. The practice of spiritual discipline is a means which leads one to godliness; it assists the believer with how to enhance his or her relationship with God. Dallas Willard writes that spiritual discipline is divided into two categories: *abstinence* and *engagement*. The *disciplines of abstinence* that Willard records are: solitude, silence, fasting, frugality, chastity, secrecy, and sacrifice. *Disciplines of engagement* are: study, worship celebration, service, prayer, fellowship, confession, and submission.[2] Each category and discipline is exampled from Dallas Willard's book on *The Spirit of the Disciplines* and listed below.

---

[2]Ibid., 158.

Disciplines of Abstinence

Disciplines of Abstinence

Solitude is choosing to be alone, a prayerful contrition on our experience of isolation from other human beings. Human interactions are capable of distorting a believer's interaction with God. Solitude allows freedom from the ingrained behaviors that may hinder a believer's integration into God's will. Prayerfully seeking God away from the crowd is just what Jesus did to hear the voice of God. When examining the life of Jesus, Christians will quickly realize that when Jesus left the crowds to be alone with the Father, great things happened when He returned. Solitude is considered the primary discipline of abstinence.

Silence is the reality of solitude. For the sake of the soul, leaving cell phones, televisions, and radios off can allow believers time to listen to God.

Listening to God can be the strongest testimony of a person of faith.

Solitude and silence must be addressed together as two disciplines that are inseparable. Jesus got up, left the house and went off to a solitary place, where he prayed (Mark 1:35, NIV). Jesus withdrawing to be alone with the Father was a catalyst to His ministry. Our Lord deliberately made time to be alone with God the Father. Jesus and the Father was never separated: the Father sent Him and is with Him (John 8:29). Jesus felt the compelling need to seek solitude.

The life of Jesus was a depiction of one who was concerned about staying perfectly in tuned to His Father's voice. His desire was to live in harmony with the will of the Father. Jesus said, "My meat [food] is to do the will of him that sent me…" (John 4:34). The Lord knew that to fulfill His purpose, to insure His steps remained ordered by the Father, He would require much time alone with God the Father. "The Lord confides in those who fear Him" (Psalm 25:14, NIV).

Solitude and silence will assist us in becoming closer to the Father, not necessarily so we can talk to Him, but so we can listen as He talks to us. In my travels from Birmingham I listen to a local station, 98.7FM, but the further I am from Birmingham, the more static interferes with me hearing the voices and the music. The static of the world often prevents us from hearing clearly the voice of the Lord. Solitude and silence keeps us on the proper frequency with the Father's voice. Jesus says. "When you pray, go into your room, close the door and pray to your Father, who is unseen" (Matt. 6:6. NIV).

Preparation Exercise (1):

What do you need to adjust in your life to align yourself with this discipline?

_____

_____

_____

_____

_____

_____

_____

_____

_____

_____

_____

_____

_____

Fasting confirms that God is a sustaining source beyond food. Jesus said, "Man shall not live by bread alone, but by every word that proceedeth out of the mouth of God" (Matthew. 4:4). Jesus is quoting from Deuteronomy 8:3. In Matthew 4:3, Satan suggests that Jesus should use His own powers to meet His own needs. Note that whenever we put our physical needs ahead of our spiritual needs, we sin. When we permit circumstances to manage and dictate our actions, rather than following God's will, we sin. Our Lord understood that His powers should never function independently of the Father's will; He came to obey the Father (John 5:30; 6:38). The Lord's aim was to defeat Satan; our aim is to honor God in every arena of our life, with every part of our existence so much so that our life will be a constant reminder to Satan that he is defeated.

Understanding what the center of the Lord's will is for your life is the object of a spiritual fast. Weight loss, your health, your family, eating; these things may be a result of your fast; however, they will never become greater than the object of your spiritual fast, understanding and living in the center of the Lord's will.

Fasting is what one does unto the Lord to later be able to feast on doing His will. The object of fasting is to understand the Lord's Will, not food or other things. Fasting is an act of humility which escorts us closer to the transforming consciousness of God's will (Rom. 12:2 & 3). Jesus teaches that fasting exposes the believer to an awareness of what he has in God. He says, "I have meat to eat that ye know not of" (Jn. 4:32). In John 4:32, the people were convinced Jesus was speaking of literal food, and they wondered where he got it. Jesus explained that doing the

Father's will, leading the woman to salvation, is nourishment for the soul. His disciples were satisfied with bread, but He was satisfied with accomplishing the Father's work.

Our creative purpose is to accomplish the Lord's will; joy is realized when we learn how to do that in the context of our life. In the book *Sermons* by Phillips Brooks and John Cotton Brooks, Phillips Brooks cites from his message titled "Make The Men Sit Down" is based on the passage in John 6:10: "Seek your life's nourishment in your life's work."[3] God's will must be the source of nourishment and satisfaction for a Christian's life.

To personally realize and understand God's will for your life is the reason for fasting. Spiritual fasting should not become a tool for weight loss; it is a biblical principle which transports one into

---

[3]Ibid., 242.

understanding God's will for his or her life. While this discipline has to do primarily with food, in a more inclusive context it is cutting out or adjusting one's lifestyle away from any craving or habit that prevents him or her from living in the Lord's will. The author of Hebrews states, "Let us lay aside every weight and sin that so easily ensnares us ..."(Hebrews 12:1).

Preparation Exercise (2):

What do you need to adjust in your life to align yourself with this discipline?

_____
_____
_____
_____
_____
_____
_____
_____
_____
_____
_____
_____
_____

Frugality is a service that is given to God and to mankind. Frugality is to abstain from using money or things that we have at disposal to merely gratify our desires for status, glamour, or luxury. This discipline, will assist one "to do justice, to love mercy, and to walk humbly with thy God" (Micah. 6:8). The discipline of frugality is not an implication that living in poverty somehow brings a person closer to God, any more than being rich keeps a person from having a relationship with Him.

God had a controversy with Israel (Micah 6:1-8); they had sinned. So the people answer God by asking how they can make up for all that they have done wrong. Their response is paraphrased: We could give sacrifices, but they can never wash away sins. Our religion can never save us. Their final response is an indication that they knew what God wanted them to do: "...*to act justly, to love faithfulness, and to walk humbly with your God"* (Micah 6:8 CSB). God does not want extravagant gifts and sacrifices; He wants our hearts.

Nathen went to David after David's affair with Bathsheba in Ps. 51:16-17(CSB). David concluded of God, *"You do not want a sacrifice, or I would give it; You are not pleased with a burnt offering. The sacrifice pleasing to God is a broken spirit. God, You will not despise a broken and humbled heart."* In Samuel's rebuke of Saul in 1 Sam. 15:22 (NIV), Samuel reminds Saul, "...Does the Lord delight in burnt offerings and sacrifices as much as in obeying the LORD? To obey is better than the fat of rams."

In Isa. 1:10-18 God reminds His people that materialism does not impress Him. He says in verse 16-18 for His people to cleanse themselves, stop doing wrong, learn to do right, seek justice, defend the oppressed, care for fatherless and plead the case of the widow. What you and I possess is not impressive to God; it is the position of our heart and how we care for those who have hardships.

However, wealth is not condemned in Scripture, but an extravagant life style may hinder one's witness to a lost world and may cause one to concentrate less on God and more on materialism and self (1 Timothy 6:10). Frugality, makes it possible to concentrate, and concentrating on "one thing is needful" (Luke 10:42). In Nehemiah 5:14-19 (CSB); Nehemiah records:

> ... from the day King Artaxerxes appointed me to be their governor in the land of Judah; from the twentieth year until his thirty-second year, 12 years; I and my associates never ate from the food allotted to the governor. The governors who preceded me had heavily burdened the people, taking food and wine from them, as well as a pound of silver. Their subordinates also oppressed the people, but I didn't do this, because of the fear of God. Instead, I devoted myself to the construction of the wall, and all my subordinates were gathered there for the work. We didn't buy any land.

What an awesome wittiness. Nehemiah not only practiced frugality, but he became an example to his people. Frugality must be practiced with wisdom and humility.

Preparation Exercise (3):

What do you need to adjust in your life to align yourself with this discipline?

_____

_____

_____

_____

_____

_____

_____

_____

_____

_____

_____

_____

_____

Chastity is an abstention from sexual gratification. We live in a culture which propitiates sexual indulgence unlike any in prior years. To honor God with your body must be your spiritual priority regardless of your personal desires or society influences. Sexual activity prior to marriage is unbiblical, not condoned by God. "Do you not know that you are God's temple and that God's Spirit dwells in you?" If anyone destroys God's temple, God will destroy that person. For God's temple is holy, and you are that temple" (1 Cor. 3:16,17 RSV).

A believer's body, life, and total being should be a representation of holiness. However, too often our churches have become playgrounds for sexual immorality and not classrooms of accountability and restoration to God. Problems of sexual immorality have permeated the local church. However, what many have failed to realize is that each of us build into the church what we have already built into our own lives. Therefore, before the local church becomes better, you and I have to become better in our relationship with God, in our marriage, and in our homes.

Chastity has an important role within a marriage: to seek the proper disposal of sexual acts, feelings, and attitudes. Sexuality cannot be paramount in a believer's life. Chastity should be practiced in conjunction with fasting and praying, and with mutual agreement (1 Corinthians 7:5).

Marriage is a place where two persons, husband and wife, are to honor God through their relationship with each other. 1 Corinthians 7:2 reminds us that God does not approve of polygamy or homosexual marriages. God's standard has always been from the beginning, one man married to one woman. The aim of chastity as a discipline is to not allow sexual gratification to be placed at the center of the marriage. This discipline focuses on loving the whole person.

However, each must note that neither husband nor wife must abuse the privilege of sexual love that is a normal part of marriage. Scripture teaches that the wife's body belongs to the husband, and the husband's body to the wife; each must be considerate of the other. Sexual love is a beautiful thing when it is used to honor each other in a marriage when both seek to honor God. Sexual love should never be used as a weapon in marriage. To refuse each other is to commit robbery (1 Thessalonians 4:6) and to invite Satan to tempt the partners to seek their satisfaction elsewhere. In everything the spiritual must govern the physical.

Preparation Exercise (4):

What do you need to adjust in your life to align yourself with this discipline?

_____
_____
_____
_____
_____
_____
_____
_____
_____
_____
_____
_____
_____
_____
_____
_____

Secrecy is to abstain from causing our good deeds to be known. Secrecy is not deceit; rather this discipline teaches how to tame one's desire for fame, justification, and attention from others. Secrecy is better accomplished through God's grace. When practiced, secrecy will assist in learning how to accept misunderstanding for the sake of peace, joy, or for the purpose of God's greater good. Secrecy is a stabilizer in the believer's faith.

In Matthew 6: 1-4, Jesus did not condemn the Pharisees for their practices of alms giving; rather he cautioned them to make sure that their hearts were right as they practiced them. Secrecy teaches us that we should never live for the praise of men; to do so is foolish and is not lasting (1 Peter 1:24). The praise of God is the only thing that should matter to the believer.

Our sinful nature can defile every good intention we have when practicing this discipline; therefore, one must be careful to insure that our motive is not to receive the praise of men but God. If our motive is to serve God and please Him, then we will give our gifts without calling attention to them or to ourselves.

The discipline of secrecy is not teaching us that it is wrong to give or practice it openly; all of our actions do not have be anonymous. In the early church everyone knew that Barnabas had given the income from the sale of his land (Acts 4:34-37). When the church members laid their money at the apostles' feet, it was not done in secret. The difference, of course, was in the motive and manner in which it was done. In contrast Ananias and Sapphire (Acts 5:1-11) tried to use their gift to make people think they were more spiritual than they really were. When practicing the discipline of secrecy, ask yourself if your motive is in tune with honoring God or are you seeking your own reward from your neighbor.

Preparation Exercise (5):

What do you need to adjust in your life to align yourself with this discipline?

_____

_____

_____

_____

_____

_____

_____

_____

_____

_____

_____

_____

_____

Sacrifice is when the believer forsakes the security of meeting needs with what is in his hands, his personal possessions. Sacrifice is a total abandonment to God, trusting on Him to meet all of your needs. Abraham knew about such abandonment when he was prepared to sacrifice Isaac. The writer of Hebrews explains (Heb. 11:19) that Abraham was actually counting upon his Lord to raise Isaac from the dead to fulfill the promise of lineage. Jesus said, while on the cross (Luke 23:46), *"Father into your hands I commend my Spirit,"* which is total sacrifice.

Sacrifice is the principle of faith. 2 Corinthians 5:7 says that *"we walk by faith";* sacrifice is also the principle of prayer – of getting things done on earth as it is in heaven (Matthew 6:10): "thy Kingdom come, thy will be done on earth as it is in heaven." Sacrifice is when a person faithfully follows God even when he or she cannot trace Him or cannot figure Him out.

One must trust His assignments by faith. Remember, God does not give us a preflight itinerary. Sacrifice is woven throughout our theology.

Also, the Old Testament writers teach that a sacrifice was a painful act to God; the person making the sacrifice had to give up, or be willing to lose something in hopes of honoring God. In our present culture we have a tendency to misappropriate this word sacrifice. We are not making a sacrifice when the act is not painful for us to achieve, and our motive fails to honor God.

Preparation Exercise (6):

What do you need to adjust in your life to align yourself with this discipline?

_____

_____

_____

_____

_____

_____

_____

_____

_____

_____

_____

_____

_____

Disciplines of Engagement

Disciplines of Engagement

In practicing spiritual discipline, a call to abstain from those things that hinder a person's commitment to God requires an engagement in things that make one a disciple. Disciplines of engagement are study, worship celebration, service, prayer, fellowship, confession, and submission.[4]

Study is the primary discipline of engagement. The discipline of study allows one to become engaged in the Word of God, both written and spoken. Any relationship one hopes to have with God will not be accomplished outside of personal study of the Word of God.

In 2 Timothy 2:15 Paul encourages Timothy to "Study to show thyself approved unto God, a workmen that needeth not to be ashamed, rightly dividing the word of truth." The word *study* means, "to

---

[4]Ibid, 158.

be diligent", zealous. Paul uses *diligent* in 2 Timothy 4:9, 21 and also in Titus 3:12.

The emphasis in 2 Timothy 2:15 is that the workman needs to be diligent in his labors so that he will not be ashamed when his work is inspected. How are you doing as it relates to your money, motives, and marriage as it relates to the Word? Will your life pass the test of God's Word? Notice in the text "rightly dividing" means "cutting straight" and can be applied to many different tasks: plowing a straight row, cutting a straight board, sewing a straight seam.

Consider this: God's Word is a plumb-line, a measuring rod for our life. Primarily, our diligence as a workman is to seek to lineup our life with God's Word. All of us as God's workmen will be either *approved* or *ashamed*. The word *approved* means "one who has been tested and found acceptable". The word was used for testing and approving metals. Each trial that we encounter forces us to study the Word to find God's will so that we will be found approved. When we diligently obey God's Word, we succeed in overcoming our trails; then, we are approved by God. Know this: that through our prayers, studying, and suffering we will not become approved unless we obey His Word.

To be ashamed means that the workman's life fails to meets God's standard and cannot pass the test or be accepted. We lose our reward when we do not pass God's inspection, when we fail to follow the Lord's specifications. Our diligence to this discipline is essential for our spiritual maturity.

Preparation Exercise (7):

What do you need to adjust in your life to align yourself with this discipline?

_____

_____

_____

_____

_____

_____

_____

_____

_____

_____

_____

_____

_____

Worship is profitable only when Jesus Christ is the center and the aim of the worship experience. Worship is to realize God's worthiness, His greatness, and to be engaged with Him in the experience (Rev. 4:11). In worship, the worshiper meets God.

In the Westminster Shorter Catechism that was completed 1647, it is recorded that "the chief end of man is to glorify God and enjoy Him forever"[5]. In 1 Peter 4:11, he records: "So that in everything God may be glorified through Jesus Christ. To Him belong the glory and the power forever and ever. Amen."

Man was created to worship. Augustine stated, "Our hearts are restless until they find rest in Thee."[6]

---

[5]The Presbyterian Church, *The Westminster Shorter Catechism* (Phil., PA; Presbyterian Church in the USA Board of Publication and Sabbath-School Work), 7.

[6]Jay P. Green, Sr., *Saint Augustine's Confessions; Saint Augustine of Hippo* (United States; Lightning Source, Inc., 2001), 1.

Also, man was redeemed to worship. Jesus said that the "Son of Man came into the world to seek and to save that which was lost" (Luke 19:10). In John 4:23 He says that the Father wants people to worship Him; here we find one of the primary reasons for worship: redemption.

Warren Wiersbe gives us a warning regarding our worship: "If we look upon worship only as a means of getting something from God, rather than giving something to God, then we make God our servant instead of our Lord, and the elements of worship become a cheap formula for selfish gratification."[7] Only in worshiping God are we doing what we are created to do and what we have been redeemed to do. To worship God is our ultimate end.

---

[7] Warren W. Wiersbe, *Real Worship; Playground, Battleground, Holy Ground* (Grand Rapids, Michigan: Baker Books, 2000), 28.

Preparation Exercise (8):

What do you need to adjust in your life to align yourself with this discipline?

_____

_____

_____

_____

_____

_____

_____

_____

_____

_____

_____

_____

_____

Celebration is often not considered among the disciplines; however, it is an important component to who we are in the Lord. You and I are people of Praise. To turn away from the world, and from those with which you formally fellowship, is necessary for believers. To learn how to be engaged with other believers in celebration is imperative for a healthy faith. Fellowship with others who know God involves relating stories of how God is actively on the move in the life of man. Miriam (Exodus 15:20), Deborah (Judges 5), and David (2 Samuel 6:12-16) are examples of the discipline of celebration. Also, the Lord's first miracle was at a wedding in Cana (John 2).

When the Lord led the horses and chariots of Pharaoh into the sea while the Israelites walked through the sea on dry ground, "***Miriam*** the prophetess, Aaron's sister took a tambourine in her hand, and all the women followed her with tambourines and dancing. Miriam sang to them: Sing to the LORD, for He is highly exalted; He has thrown the horse and its rider into the sea" (Exodus 15: 20, 21 CSB).

When the Israelites destroyed King Jabin of Canaan, **Deborah** broke out in a song, which is recorded in Judges 5. In 2 Samuel 6 **David** received word that the Lord had blessed the household of Obed-edom and all those who belonged to him because of the ark of God. David went and brought up the ark of God rejoicing, dancing and shouting.

Scripture teaches that the discipline of celebration is a public expression of praise to God for His blessings. The discipline of celebration when practiced can be a witness of God's goodness to a lost world. You and I must share what God is doing in us and around us to a lost world. I believe God will always show us when and with whom to share this discipline.

Preparation Exercise (9):

What do you need to adjust in your life to align yourself with this discipline?

_____
_____
_____
_____
_____
_____
_____
_____
_____
_____
_____
_____
_____
_____

Service: the discipline of service helps us to realize and respond to needs of those we encounter (Matthew 20:25-28). This discipline teaches that responding to God's moments of opportunity often takes us away from our personal agenda, those things we may have recorded on the calendar. To live as a servant while doing ministry and fulfilling a social role is the greatest challenge a believer may face, especially if his ministry context is the low income or socially and economically deprived. To be a servant in ministry means that ministry and our social role while in culture are both interrelated, the servant of God is never devoid of the culture he or she serves; this is ministry at its finest. As a servant you and I are called to minister from a duel exegete, both text and culture. One most not love one and ignore the other.

Preparation Exercise (10):

What do you need to adjust in your life to align yourself with this discipline?

_____

_____

_____

_____

_____

_____

_____

_____

_____

_____

_____

_____

_____

Prayer: the most defining discipline that a believer has is prayer. Conversing with God in prayer opens an opportunity for the believer to experience crucibles in his life and in ministry. Crucibles are defining moments in a person's life which change him or her forever; we often remember these moments for the rest of our life. Prayer is always aligned with other disciplines and assists the believer in becoming victorious over the enemy. In the Garden of Gethsemane, the Lord calls for His disciples to *watch and pray.* Prayer is one of but a few disciplines that is capable of strengthening a believer's faith. But, it must be done without ceasing (1 Th.5:17; Phi. 4:6).

In his writings on the *Power In Prayer* published in the Northfield Echoes, Volume 4, Dwight L. Moody cites that you and I must: "Spread out your petition before God, and then say, Thy will, not mine, be done. The sweetest lesson I have learned in God's school is to let the Lord choose for me."[8] Notice how the Apostle Paul expresses his passion for prayer below; every believer should be this passionate about his or her prayer life: "Be careful for nothing; but in everything by prayer and supplication with thanksgiving let your requests be made known unto God" (Philippians 4:6 KJV), or "Don't worry about anything, but in everything, through prayer and petition with thanksgiving, let your requests be made known to God" (Philippians 4:6 CSB), or "Don't fret or worry. Instead of worrying, pray. Let petitions and praises shape your worries into prayers, letting God know your concerns" (Philippians 4:6 MSG).

In the words of Phillips Brooks, "A prayer, in its simplest definition, is merely a wish turned heaven

---

[8]D. L. Moody, "Power in Prayer," in *Northfield Echoes*, Volume 4, Edited by Delavan L. Pierson (East Northfield, Mass: Northfield Echoes, 1897), 51.

ward."[9] I define prayer as a petition of *an acknowledgement, appeal, desire, an expression or confession of our faith* made to the Lord God of Heaven and Earth for His Will to be made manifest (apparent) in us and around about us, on earth as it is in heaven. John Piper in his book *Let The Nations Be Glad; The Supremacy Of God In Missions* writes:

> Life is war. That's not all it is. But it is always that. Our weakness in prayer is owing largely to our neglect of this truth. Prayer is primarily a wartime walkie-talkie for the mission of the church as it advances against the powers of darkness and unbelief. It is not surprising that prayer malfunctions when we try to make it a domestic intercom to call upstairs for more comforts in the den. God has given us prayer as a wartime walkie-talkie so that we can call headquarters for everything we need as the kingdom off Christ advances in the world. Prayer gives us the significance of front-line forces, and gives *God* the glory of a limitless Provider. The one who gives the power gets the glory. Thus prayer safeguards the supremacy of God in

---

[9]Francis Nathan Peloubet, Mary Abby Peloubet, *Select Notes: A Commentary on the International Lessons, Volume 38* (Boston, MA.: W. A. Wilde Co.,1912), 174.

missions while linking us with endless grace for every need.[10]

God wants His glory to occur in and through each Christian; therefore, we must be known by our prayers, our ability to not just talk to God but talk with God. In 2 Timothy 4:7 Paul writes, "I have fought the good fight, I have finished the race, I have kept the faith." Also, the word "fight" in 1 Timothy means to "agonize," which is used repeatedly in describing the Christian life. Paul's whole life, his proclamation of gospel and teaching is a representation of a person involved in a battle: "For this I toil, *striving* with all the energy which he mightily inspires within me" (Colossians 1:29). Paul continues by saying that prayer is part of this fight: "Epaphras, a servant of Christ and one of your own, greets you, always *striving* on your behalf in prayers" (Colossians 4:12). Paul also states, "*Strive* with me in your prayers on my behalf to God" (Romans 15:30). *Strive* is the same word used in the Greek for "fight".

---

[10]John Piper, *Let The Nation Be Glad! The Supremacy of God in Missions* (Grand Rapids, Michigan: Baker Books, 1993), 41.

Until one feels the negative effects from a life inundated with war, one will not pray as he or she ought; while marriages are being attacked, and homes are being destroyed, the spiritual and moral compasses of too many Christians have become dysfunctional by the enemy (Satan). Too many Christians have become lulled into a false sense of thinking that the enemy will not attack them because they are committed to Christ. Know that the enemy is not concerned with you; he is concerned with destroying who and what you represent, God.

In Ephesians 6:17-18 Paul draws a parallel to the Christians life of war and the work of prayer: "And take the helmet of salvation, and the sword of the Spirit which is the word of God: Praying always with all prayer and supplication in the Spirit, and watching thereunto with all perseverance and supplication for all saints." Verses 17 and 18 are connected in the Greek which implies that each verse is breathed together by the Holy Spirit, which means they are interrelated, interdependent to each other. The Word of God and Prayer are two wings on the same bird; survival in this Christian battle depends on understanding and applying this dualism to one's life.

Piper states, "Prayer is the communication with headquarters by which the weapons of warfare are deployed according to the will of God. That's the connection between the weapons and prayer in Ephesians 6. Prayer is for war."[11] A review of scripture reveals that prayer is universal. Prayer is not confined to geographical, cultural, or ethnic barriers. To understand this, one must realize that the foundation of our prayers rest in the sovereignty of God. All things are under the rule and control of God. Thus, nothing happens to us, good or bad as things may seem, absent from the sovereignty of God. Nothing takes God by surprise. Our prayers will have little or no meaning unless we take into account the *character, nature,* and the *sovereignty* of God.

T. W. Hunt, author of *The Doctrine of Prayer* writes, "Prayer must be built on the foundation of the sovereignty and character of God. Prayer is as old as man, permeates all of history, and is common to all people. Scripturally, prayer is universal in time, in space, and in the scope of its content."[12] Prayer

---

[11]Ibid, 45.

[12]T.W. Hunt, *The Doctrine of Prayer* (Nashville, Tennessee: Convention Press, 1986), 8.

discharges our desires into the hands, mind, and will of a sovereign Heavenly Father who cares about everyone.

Prayer is universal throughout *time*. Men called on the Lord from the beginning of creation realizing their fragility and need for God. The greatest men and women – Moses, Abraham, Hannah, and Mary -- were people of prayer. The lives of biblical saints of God from Genesis to Malachi, from Matthew to Revelation, were characterized by prayer.

Prayer is also universal in *space.* Prayer crosses all geographical, racial, or ethnic lines. The word *all* is one of the most important words in the Bible. The psalmist sings, "O Thou who dost hear prayer, to Thee all men come" (Ps. 65:2). Jesus declared, "I, if I be lifted up from the earth, will draw all men to Myself" (John 12:32). Therefore, Paul could write in Romans 10:13, "Whoever will call upon the name of the Lord will be saved." In Kings 8:41-43 Solomon prayed for the day when all people of the earth would know and fear Jehovah. Psalm 86:9 predicts a universal worship of the one true God: All nations whom Thou hast made shall come and worship before Thee, O Lord, and they shall glorify thy name".

Scripture teaches us that prayer is encouraged by our Lord Jesus Christ; when practiced, our prayers are capable of achieving limitless results. "Ask, and it shall be given to you; seek, and you shall find; knock, and it shall be opened to you. For everyone who asks receives, and he who seeks finds, and to him who knocks it shall be opened"(Matt. 7:7-8).

Due to our human nature, we are fallible, imperfect creatures; mistakes will occur. Therefore, our need to pray and seek the Lord's wisdom and direction is an imperative. "If any lack wisdom, let him ask of God" (James 1:5).

King Solomon was a young leader who felt that he lacked wisdom to judge Israel, so he prayed to God (1 Kings 3:3ff.). Solomon applied wisdom by making a prayer request to God for direction and discernment. As God's servant, every area of one's life must be centered on petitioning God for direction: ask, seek, and knock. God is faithful and just. He is waiting, able to meet your needs if you would only ask. The great evangelist Billy Graham is cited by Timo Pokki in his book *America's Preacher and His*

Message: Billy Graham's View of Conversion and Sanctification, "Heaven is full of answers to prayer for which no one ever bothered to ask."[13]

One's prayer life is not an accomplishment to achieve, as important as it is; rather it should be viewed as a journey, a process of growth, not a goal that is completed and set aside. Each part of a person's life is measured by his or her journey with God in prayer. However, much of what we do as Christians is not seasoned in prayer. We worship in our churches, we sing in choirs or praise teams, and often make life altering decisions without consulting God in prayer. Paul exhorts the Thessalonians in First Thessalonians 5:17 & 18, "Pray constantly. Give thanks in everything for this is God's will for you in Christ Jesus." Our walk with God is not an event but a journey of prayer; it's not an achievement but a constant prayer process with God which provides direction for life.

---

[13] Timo Pokki, *America's Preacher and His Message: Billy Graham's View of Conversion and Sanctification* (Lanham, Maryland: University Press of America, Inc., 1999), 206.

ST. FRANCIS' PRAYER

Lord, make me an instrument of Thy peace.

Where there is hate, may I bring love;

Where offense, may I bring pardon;

May I bring union in place of discord;

Truth, replacing error;

Faith, where once there was doubt;

Hope, for despair;

Light, where was darkness;

Joy to replace sadness.

Make me not to so crave to be loved as to love.

Help me to learn that in giving I may receive;

In forgetting self, I may find life eternal.

(St. Francis of Assisi)

Prayer is a petition to God. The *Pray-er is* the person who prays, a word in English that embodies the act of the *pray-er:* you and I, our heritage *prayer*, and our relationship with the Father. So then one's *prayer* life is his or her spiritual DNA. You are a *prayer*, identifiable by your *prayer* journey which should always be to glorify our heavenly Father.

Regardless of your trails, your encounters, know that Satan attacks your witness for God; therefore, your prayer journey must become a tool to protect your witness, and to glorify God. Jesus taught, *"Whatever you ask in my name, I will do it, that the Father may be glorified in the Son" (John 14:13).* Observe in John 16:24 Jesus says, "Till now you have asked nothing in my name; ask, and you will receive that your joy may be full." Each of the above passages presents a dual purpose for prayer: that the Father be glorified and that our joy may be full.

Jesus tells us how to glorify God in John 15:7, "If you abide in me, and my words abide in you, ask whatever you will and it shall be done for you." When we ask God in prayer to move on our behalf through Christ, He will bring an increase in our life by taking us from *fruit* to *much fruit.* Prayer is God's power acting on our behalf. Christians must learn to seek the Lord in prayer for everything.

Preparation Exercise (11):

What do you need to adjust in your life to align yourself with this discipline?

_____
_____
_____
_____
_____
_____
_____
_____
_____
_____
_____
_____
_____

Confession: James records, "Confess your faults one to another, and pray one for another, that ye may be healed. The effectual fervent prayer of a righteous man availeth much" (Jas. 5:16). Unconfessed sin obstructs the believer's life and is trouble to the ministry of any believer. In order to practice the discipline of confession, the believer will have to divulge his weakness and failures to a person he can trust, a person that will pray for him and hold him accountable before God, i.e., a spouse or a close friend. Be prayerful about the person you select; the spiritual maturity of this person is vital. When selecting a person to confide in, three things are important:

1. The person must have a deep relationship with God.

2. One must have a deep trust and relationship with this person.
   (Time may not dictate this, only the Lord) This person may be one that is a new friend or newly established relationship, or it can be

someone that is a long-time friend or acquaintance.

3. Seek the Lord in prayer regarding the person to confide in.

Preparation Exercise (12):

What do you need to adjust in your life to align yourself with this discipline?

_____

_____

_____

_____

_____

_____

_____

_____

_____

_____

_____

_____

_____

Submission: every discipline that is practiced by the believer is sustained by the discipline of submission. The believer's ability to lead is defined by how well he is able to submit. His submission serves as an example to the flock: "Be shepherds of God's flock that is under your care, watching over them -- not because you must, but because you are willing, as God wants you to be; not pursuing dishonest gain, but eager to serve; not lording it over those entrusted to you, but being examples to the flock" (1 Pet. 5:2-3, NIV). Submission is not obedience. Rather, submission is a voluntary act of allegiance, support, and response to another based on a single objective: to represent and honor the Lord in all that you seek to accomplish.

The discipline of submission, when practiced, assists the believer to recognize those who are capable of pouring into his life. Paul recognizes mutual submission of all to all: "Submit to one another out of reverence for Christ" (Eph. 5:21, NIV). In Philippians Paul also states, "Instead of being motivated by selfish ambition or vanity, each of you should, in humility, be moved to treat one another as more important than yourself" (Philippians. 2:3, Net Bible). God honors those who put His glory before their own.

Preparation Exercise (13):

What do you need to adjust in your life to align yourself with this discipline?

Conclusion

The practice of Spiritual disciplines assists believers with guarding their witness and character and enhancing their faith. Spiritual discipline will also highlight the frustrations that may harm a person's walk with God. Faithfully committing one's life to the practice of these disciplines will result in a clearer understanding of God's will for his or her life. I pray that you will continue your journey of *Practicing Spiritual Disciplines.* A good place to start would be *Master Life* by Avery T. Willis, Jr. and Kay Moore.

Prayer Journal & Note Guide

Bibliography

Brooks. Phillips and John Cotton Brooks. *Sermons! Visions and Tasks*. New York: E. P.
   Dutton & Company, 1886.

Green. Jay P. Sr. *Saint Augustine's Confessions; Saint Augustine of Hippo*. United
   States: Lightning Source, Inc., 2001.

Hunt. T.W. *The Doctrine of Prayer*. Nashville, Tennessee: Convention Press, 1986.

Moody. D. L. "Power in Prayer," in *Northfield Echoes*, Volume 4. Edited by Delavan L.
   Pierson East Northfield, Mass: Northfield Echoes, 1897.

Peloubet, Francis Nathan and Mary Abby Peloubet, *Select Notes: A Commentary on*
   the International Lessons, Volume 38. Boston, MA.: W. A. Wilde Co.,1912.

Piper. John. *Let The Nation Be Glad! The Supremacy of God in Missions*. Grand
   Rapids, Michigan: Baker Books, 1993.

Pokki. Timo. *America's Preacher and His Message: Billy Graham's View of Conversion
   and Sanctification.* Lanham, Maryland: University Press of America, Inc., 1999.

The Presbyterian Church, *The Westminster Shorter Catechism*. Phil., PA; Presbyterian.
   Church in the USA Board of Publication and Sabbath-School Work

Wiersbe. Warren W. *Real Worship; Playground, Battleground, Holy Ground*. Grand
    Rapids, Michigan: Baker Books, 2000.

Willard, Dallas. *The Spirit of the Disciplines*. San Francisco: Harper Collins Publishers,
    2009.

Made in the USA
Columbia, SC
04 July 2017